CORE VALUES

By Ian Livingstone

Dedicated to All Who Love America
....and to Abigail for her future

Acknowledgements

I acknowledge all my teachers and the genius of those whose ideas I have studied. I claim no ownership of the ideas in this book but am privileged to shape them in a way that expresses my love for this country.

CONTENTS

INTRODUCTION

America will never be destroyed from the outside. If we falter and lose our freedoms, it will be because we destroyed ourselves.

~ Abraham Lincoln

Are you angry at what's happening to our country? Do you feel frustrated and helpless to change things or to have your voice heard? Do you sense that your cherished values are being attacked and stripped away from you? Is your individuality being devalued? Is your incentive to work and profit by your work being squashed? Are we squandering our national treasure and jeopardizing our children's future? Have we become unwitting allies to our enemies who seek to destroy us?

If you feel these things in your heart and in your gut and not just in your mind, then your core or soul is letting you know that we are going in the wrong direction. As a nation, we are moving against the stream of life, away from fulfillment and strength.

We, the people, were asleep at the wheel while the campaign against our soul-derived values accelerated. We only stirred from our stupor when the destructiveness of the extreme liberal agenda had reached alarming proportions. As a nation, we handed over responsibility for our freedom and protection to those we did not know. We traded our freedom for the illusion of peace and security, for being taken care of. We entrusted the safekeeping of our core values to strangers.

We tell our children not to trust strangers. Then, why do we trust strangers in Washington to do what is right for us and for children's future? We shouldn't trust these people unless we understand how they view the world and how close they are, in their hearts and minds, to truly valuing life and individual freedom.

We may have been asleep, but we're not stupid, and we can learn from our mistakes if we understand ourselves and how the conservative and liberal person views the world.

We need to know who to trust with our freedom and future. We can only do so by seeing their character and knowing if they share our deepest values. Otherwise we'll repeat the same mistakes, whatever political party is in power.

The framers of our Constitution functioned from their core. Liberal and conservative alike, they clustered around a deep abiding respect for life, liberty and individual expression of that life. The same core, from which our founding fathers drew, is available to us if we know what we are looking for and where to find it.

This book defines what our core values are and identifies the source of these values as our God-given life and our impulse to protect this precious life. We will learn why some people are liberal and others conservative and how the balance between the conservative and liberal which once strengthened our nation has been upset and now polarizes and weakens us. We will understand why some of us cherish the individual expression of life while others want to collectivize it. The following chapters reveal why some individuals worship the intellect while others retain feeling for life in all its manifestations and explains why so many people demand freedom but won't accept the personal responsibility that accompanies that freedom. We will come to realize that sensitivity is not weakness and that aggression and strength are appropriate to protect life and liberty.

Most importantly, we will learn to identify the motives and means of operation of those who seek to supplant our core values with destructive and divisive values. Once we see the intentions and modus operandi of the extremist, the person who wants to bend the world to his will, we will know how best to respond. Without such understanding, we lash out blindly in reaction to that which threatens us, or we retreat and live in fear and confusion.

The gains of the 2010 mid-term election are only a start to reversing the destructive tide of extreme liberal policies. This is not a time for complacency. The fate and direction of our country hangs in the balance. We are in danger of repeating past mistakes unless we draw from our core strength, compare everything to our core values and open our eyes to political character.

Anyone who has ever felt the pulse of life in themselves, in nature, who has recognized the same life in their neighbor and acknowledged their God, belongs with us in the fight to express our individuality and to abide by our core values.

PART I

KNOWING OUR CORE VALUES

King Solomon said:
Wisdom is the principal thing; therefore get wisdom: and with all thy get-
ting get understanding

~ Proverbs 4:7

We can best protect our core values by understanding ourselves as well as by understanding those who seek to pull us as far as possible from our central values. Unless we know what makes each of us tick we will fall into the trap of reacting blindly to the extreme liberal agenda.

CHAPTER 1
WHAT IS OUR CORE?
THE BASIS FOR BEING A STRONG INDIVIDUAL

Men cannot abandon their religious faith without a kind of aberration of intellect and a sort of violent distortion of their true nature; they are invincibly brought back to more pious sentiments. Unbelief is an accident, and faith is the only permanent state of mankind.

~ Alexis de Tocqueville

To fully appreciate our core values, we first need to know where these values come from and what our core really is.

What is my core?

Our God-given life is found deep within our being. It doesn't matter what we call it for it has many names such as essence, soul, inner being. I refer to this center of life as our core.

Where is it to be found?

We will find it where we feel it most, in our heart and gut. As a neurologist, and contrary to popular belief, I firmly believe that our brain is not our epicenter. Our core makes itself known by feeling, not by thinking – that "gut feeling", the warmth in our heart when we know something is right comes from our core. Too much thinking obscures its message.

Belief, hardwiring and character

What we believe determines how we see ourselves and how we view the world around us. The human brain is hardwired for belief.

There are ten times as many neural pathways for top-down reasoning (where a premise or belief determines what we perceive and what motivates our actions) than there are for bottom-up or inductive reasoning (where we begin with an observation and then build up a theory or hypothesis). Top-down reasoning is the way of faith, and inductive reasoning is the mind of science.

The Bible tells us about the power of faith and belief. We are free to choose what we want to believe and what we demonstrate in our lives is, to a large degree, a result of what we believe. It is up to each one of us to realize as much of our potential as we can. If we believe we are able to achieve something, then we will most likely realize our goal. On the other hand, if we see ourselves as helpless and inferior, our belief will be carried downstream into poorer outcomes. The battle for control of our political opinion is really a grab to try and turn our beliefs from one thing to another. For example, we are asked to believe that big government is the answer to our problems and to give up our belief that we, as individuals, should solve our own problems and be responsible for our own actions. Our success in preventing others from imposing their beliefs and opinions on us depends largely on how much we prize our individuality and this, in turn, depends on how anchored we are in our core values. As we shall see, the liberal and the conservative person each see the world through the lens of their own beliefs.

Our brain circuitry determines our personality and character. A creative artist, a shy person, a brash dogged nature, a stubborn individual or a goal-driven person are all determined, to some degree, by this wiring.

Just as our wiring determines our personality and individuality, it also determines how we view and respond to the society in which we live, why some of us are conservative while others are liberal.

This is not to say any one is good or other bad, these are just fundamental differences in how we view the society in which we live. Ideas and thoughts come and go but our character is deeply etched in our brains and remains for life having been molded by our upbringing and life experience and is fully formed by early adulthood.

Now, let us put this brain circuitry, this hardwiring into perspective.

We function as though we have three basic layers:

> 1. Our core: At the center of our being lies intelligent, loving, pure life.

> 2. Middle layer: This is the layer of all the circuitry and wiring by which the core impulses are perceived and expressed. The healthier we are, the more clearly we perceive and feel our core impulses. The denser and darker this middle layer becomes, the less the person is aware of his core and the more distorted his core impulses become when expressed. This is the dark side of human nature. It's the layer that contains hate, brutality and is also the layer of fear.

> 3. Surface layer: This is the veneer, the thin polish of personality, the mask that we present to the world. This often hides the ugly middle layer.

From this schema, we can see how our core lies deep within us. Some people have their core so deeply obscured that they function almost exclusively from the dark middle layer while in others their core is bright and shines through to the surface.

These three layers are not actually physical layers. You cannot see them, but they are very real, and they play out in our lives.

What are the qualities of a person living from his core? I think Jesus Christ represents what it is like to live completely from one's core because of his openness, his love of life in all its manifestations and his support of the individual while he also retained a natural aggression against those who desecrate life, such as the money changers in the temple. Most of us obviously fall short of this ideal, but in varying degrees. On the other extreme, those hate-filled individuals, like the Jihadists, that seek to destroy others and impose their life-negating will on their fellow man are functioning from the dark middle layer and have no access at all to their core.

Our core is accessed only by feeling. Feeling comes first, thoughts follow. When we function from the core, our brain and intellect serves life, serves to express our core and not the other way around. This, as we shall see, is one of the fundamental differences between the conservative, who prioritizes feeling from the core, and the liberal, whose intellect tends to separate him from his core.

As mentioned earlier, conservative and liberal represent a healthy balance in society just as feeling and reason, emotion and intellect are necessary for a healthy balance in the individual. Relying too much on feeling and moving away from reasoning leads to irrational actions just as over- intellectualization without feeling is unhealthy. This is discussed in more detail in Chapters 3 and 4.

Chapter 2
What are Core Values?

We hold these truths to be self-evident, that all men are created equal, that they are endowed by their Creator with certain unalienable rights, that among these are life, liberty and the pursuit of happiness.

The Declaration of Independence shows our forefathers valued the right to live from their core. It demonstrated they accepted the responsibility for doing so and would fight, to the last breath, for each person's right to express his core in his own way.

Feelings from our core include:

- Feeling of belonging, being part of life and nature
- Religious feeling, acknowledging an inner wisdom, a power higher than our own self
- Love and respect for life
- Respect for the individual
- Love of freedom and liberty but not without responsibility
- Simplicity rather than complexity
- Love of work
- Custody and a sense of responsibility for the environment
- Belief in the intrinsic goodness of man but with the ability to recognize and respond to the destructive impulse in others
- Curiosity and thirst for knowledge

Living from your core gives you a feeling of independence and individuality. Feelings from the core give rise to spontaneous gratitude for being alive, not just for circumstances or material things, but for life itself. From this springs love, the recognition of life in ourselves, in others and in nature and the desire to respect and support that life in all its individual manifestations. From this core comes a belief in freedom, liberty, justice and peace for all. The core individual is self-reliant and accepts the responsibility for his own welfare. The core individual will not give away his freedom in order to be taken care of by the welfare state.

This core is also the source of strength and rational aggression to protect life, particularly when it is vulnerable. This aggression is not destructive. It is the same aggressive impulse a mother bear feels when her cub is threatened.

The capacity to work is a significant core function. It is a major source of fulfillment and one of the essential functions of human endeavor. Giving value and receiving value in turn, exchange, recognition, responsibility are all part of core work function. The recklessness of government in encouraging dependency, devaluing work by removing incentive, and by redistributing and squandering the nation's wealth is what happens when economic policy is stripped away from the core.

In summary, core impulses give us a sense of belonging, of strength, of being individual, of valuing freedom, of loving life coupled with responsibility and religious feeling.

The impulses of life from the core can be distorted by ideologies which make everything complicated. As a general rule of thumb, the closer to truth you are, the more simple things are. Conversely, the further from truth, the more complicated and complex things become. I think of this like the solid and simple trunk of the tree through which the sap of life flows. The fractal patterns of branching, the small multiple twigs become ever more complicated the further they are from the source. Jesus used the analogy of the vine to point out that the sap, the life that nourishes each individual twig flows from a single uncomplicated source, which he called the "father".

A Note on Work and Our Core: The relationship of our core to our work deserves particular mention because it is so vital to our well-being and happiness.

Our desire to be creative, our impulse to be inventive and productive comes from our core. When our impulse to work is undistorted and unrestricted, it gives us pleasure and a feeling of fulfillment. We recognize this by the satisfaction and the value we place in our efforts and by the compensation or value we receive in return as others appreciate the work we do.

In a perfect world of core-functioning people there would be no need for regulation and rules to govern work because our function would always be life-positive – always building up, adding value and beauty to the world. As we know all too well, the world is not perfect, so rules and restrictions are needed to protect our core functions. We need protection against exploitation, excessive greed, theft and so on.

The point I want to make is that working from the core goes beyond making a living, beyond putting food on the table. Our sense of pride, value and fulfillment in work comes from the same core function whatever our work may be, be it a janitor or a brain surgeon.

When our efforts are devalued and the fruits of our labors are confiscated, our capacity to work becomes disturbed. When our core no longer has room to be innovative and creative, our economic productivity begins to die.

Economics is a complex science, but the essence, the core function, of work is simple and essential to our emotional, spiritual and material well-being. The role of government, as intended by our founding fathers, is to protect this core function, not to kill it!

Our core values are the values that we place on the feelings and impulses that arise from the mainspring of our being and the measures we take to protect that center of life within ourselves and others. In other words, core values flow directly from core feelings and include:

- value of freedom and liberty but not without responsibility
- strength and resolve to protect the core
- placing value on the core of others (loving your neighbor as your self)
- value of work
- respect for the individual
- attitude of live and let live
- no desire to impose your will or opinions on others
- independence
- feeling of custodianship and responsibility for the environment
- the ability to recognize and respond to the destructive actions of others

- respect for the life-positive beliefs of others, including their religious beliefs

- love and respect for life in all its manifestations

Government, when based on these values, serves to protect the core of each citizen and the core of the nation as a whole. The function of government is that simple. Using protection of core as a yardstick, we can see how far our nation has strayed from the ideals of our founding fathers. The Obama administration's erosion of our defenses at home and abroad is an example of exposing rather than protecting our core.

Let us now look at what the conservative and liberal character does with his core impulses. Dr. E. F. Baker, a psychiatrist, was the first person to describe the liberal and conservative character as distinct from the ideas that each character may hold. Our character comes from the hardwiring in our nervous system and determines how we see the world and what we do with our core impulses. Many conservative characters hold liberal views, which they imbibe from their environment. Fewer liberal characters hold conservative views. So, when I refer to conservative and liberal character I mean the hardwiring, not the ideas, political agendas or ideologies.

Political ideologies confuse us because we don't know ourselves. We don't always know why some ideas appeal to us while others are repulsive. The next two chapters help us to distinguish between the person and the ideas he holds. We begin with the conservative character who is the more straightforward and easier to understand of the two political character types.

CHAPTER 3
THE CONSERVATIVE CHARACTER

Man, know thyself.

~ Ancient Greek aphorism

The conservative stands just to the right of core.

To conserve is to maintain status quo. Conservatives want to maintain tradition in personal as well as political life. Therefore, conservatives are often seen as being resistant to change. William F. Buckley Jr. described this aspect of the conservative by saying "A conservative is a fellow who is standing athwart history yelling 'Stop!'"

The essential difference between the conservative and liberal character is that the conservative retains significant feeling from his core even though his perception of his core may be not always be clear.

Thus, the conservative values feeling over intellect and, as a result, is often regarded with disdain by the intellectual liberal.

The conservative thus has less contempt for his fellow man than the liberal. The conservative respects authority both within the family and in society. He respects law enforcement, and laws of the country and, ultimately the Constitution.

The conservative character has a strong sense of personal responsibility. The conservative values freedom and independence but accepts the responsibility that this freedom entails. He knows that freedom and responsibility are two sides of the same coin.

The conservative would choose freedom over personal security. He would rather accept the consequences of its own actions than be taken care of by the government. The conservative sees that each person is responsible for his own life and that although not everyone has equal abilities each person has the right to make the most of the freedom and opportunity this country offers. He accepts that not everyone turns out equal and that it is not the responsibility of the state to ensure that everyone is equally successful.

The conservative values reward for hard work and the right to reap that reward. He is, basically, at home in the capitalist system. He believes in charity as long as he can choose who will benefit from his giving.

Many conservatives reflect prevailing liberal ideas from their environment. This does not mean they're not conservative because their basic conservative structure does not prevent them from accepting and acting on liberal ideas. This is why some Republicans are liberal characters just as, less frequently, some Democrats are conservative characters. As a rule, as people become older and more life-experienced, they tend to revert more to the ideas that are consonant with their character. In other words, older conservatives are less likely to accept liberal agendas.

Chapter 4
The Liberal Character

Character is higher than intellect.

~ Ralph Waldo Emerson

The liberal stands just to the left of core and often considers himself to be smarter than the conservative. But, is this the case? This chapter explains why the liberal character tends to be so intellectual.

The liberal character was born out of a logical reaction to the excessive use of authority and extreme conservatism, such as the brutal inquisition of the Middle Ages. Liberalism led to the Age of Enlightenment and to the Renaissance.

The liberal character relies strongly on his mind, and his intellect is often overdeveloped leading to progressive loss of contact with his core feelings. The liberal is idealistic and likes to see the "good" in people. Liberals are usually good people with well-meaning intentions. They genuinely desire the best for their fellow man.

The liberal believes that the body is controlled by the brain and, as a logical extension of this belief, he believes in a central control of society much as the brain controls the body. He believes that this central control benefits everybody. The liberal stresses the importance of fair play and an even playing field.

One of the liberal character's failings is that he cannot comprehend the destructive impulses that arise from the middle layer of those who are evil, such as terrorists. The liberal character does not distinguish between healthy aggression that arises from the core and destructive, hate-driven aggression that comes from the middle layer. He believes that everyone is amenable to goodwill and all problems can be successfully negotiated through talk and compromise. He favors appeasement because he cannot tolerate aggression. He rejects the use of force and would rather favor "talks" or sanctions than confront hate-filled or destructive people. The same appeasement that Neville Chamberlain showed to Hitler in 1939 is seen in the Obama administration's policies such as appeasement with a potentially nuclear-armed Iran that leaves us open to political blackmail. The intellectual response to evil in others cannot stop human destructiveness. This is seen by our enemies, both foreign and domestic, as weakness to be exploited.

The liberal character lives in a world of words and concepts. This intellectual approach attracts him to work in the media. This is one reason why liberal characters dominate journalism and why academia is largely populated by liberal characters. The term "talking head" describes the liberal character well - an expert full of concepts ideas, clever logic, brilliant but distant from his core.

Because the liberal's feelings from his core are reduced, the liberal has diminished regard for genuine religious feeling.

The liberal's reluctance to confront the destructive impulse in others accounts for the paradox of why he will accommodate fundamentalist Islam, where religion and the state are one, yet at the same time the feels strongly about keeping church and state separate at home.

A nice summary of the differences between conservative and liberal, as quoted by Dr. E.F. Baker, was described by James Burnham in his book "Suicide of the West":

"The goals for the conservative are freedom, liberty, justice and peace in that order. For the Liberal the order of importance is exactly reversed: peace, justice, liberty, freedom. The liberal prizes justice and peace and is willing to make many concessions to freedom for the sake of peace."

Because he is less anchored in his core, the liberal character is easily swayed and influenced by the extreme liberal who functions further away from core values and who poses as a genuine, healthier liberal.

The shift of American society from core to increasingly liberal has been in progress since the 1960s. This shift has resulted in the loss of balance between liberal and conservative.

CHAPTER 5
THE LOSS OF BALANCE BETWEEN LIBERAL AND CONSERVATIVE

A house divided against itself cannot stand.

~ Abraham Lincoln

Our country is seriously out of balance, and we need to know what went wrong so that we can correct it. This chapter explains how our society has moved away from its core to the left and why liberal and conservative characters are at each other's throats rather than cooperating for the common good.

Let us start with the balance between conservative and liberal and why our nation has shifted away from its core.

Loss of Balance between the Conservative and Liberal Character

The liberal and conservative characters are neither good nor bad. As long as liberals and conservatives don't stray too far from the center and lose contact with their core, their differences create a healthy balance.

It is like the statistical phenomenon of regression to the mean where a tendency to stray to one side or the other is corrected by a return to the middle. This swing of the pendulum between conservative and liberal in a healthy society is small. As the arc become wider, the reaction of liberal to conservative and conservative to liberal becomes less healthy as society moves further from the center.

The reality is that the natural balance between conservative and liberal has shifted. Since the 1960s, our society has progressively moved to a more liberal way of thinking. The momentum toward liberalism recently accelerated, moving our country further to the left and away from our core. We are beginning to see the destructive effect of this loss of balance as revealed by a social and political agenda that is alarmingly distant from the core values on which our nation was founded.

I arrived in America, a new immigrant from a country which, at that time, was not free, in time to witness an example of the greatest transfer of power on earth: the peaceful transition from liberal to conservative as Jimmy Carter handed over the Presidency of the United States to Ronald Reagan. This powerful spectacle symbolized what had been fought for and paid for in blood – namely the power of the people embodied in the laws and Constitution of the United States. I watched in awe as I saw the sadness in Carter's face. He had his chance and bowed to the will of his people. I noted the resolve and flush of renewed hope in Reagan's demeanor as he took up the mantle the people now trusted to him.

The swearing-in ceremony symbolized the delicate and healthy balance between liberal and conservative that keeps our society whole and vibrant. It was the will of the people that had been expressed in every presidential inauguration since George Washington handed over the reins of power to John Adams.

The healthy balance between conservative and liberal keeps us vibrant, dynamic and open to options. This balance, which allows for debate and the respect for differing opinions, is only healthy when it is centered on core values. As we move into our heads ignoring our hearts, we stray away from the feelings that emanate from our core, the repository of our strength and become weaker. We begin to feel adrift in a realm of conflicting ideas as we start losing contact with our core feelings, which infallibly guide us to right action.

The rapid shift to the left of center and, consequently, the distancing between conservative and liberal viewpoints, divides our society. Everything becomes politicized as politics pervades and contaminates almost everything in our lives. We become polarized into extremes. The center is lost, the common good is forgotten, as liberals and conservatives vie with each other.

Liberal and conservative characters are not restricted to the Democratic and Republican political parties respectively.

There are some Democrats who are conservative by character but who hold liberal views, and there are liberal Republicans who hold middle of the road views. Thus it is important to not judge a political official or candidate by their party affiliation but to look at his character. The Tea Party movement recognizes the importance of character above all other political identification and credentialing. That is why the Tea Party movement is so threatening to those in the political establishment who are vulnerable because they have lost contact with their core – or never had it to begin with.

It's not too late to reestablish this balance, but the only way to do so is to recognize what is happening - and why - and to follow the guiding star of our core values back to center.

Our Shift to the Left

Our shift to the left that began in the 1960s has accelerated dramatically in the past few years moving us further and further away from core functioning and transforming us from a robust, core-centered nation into an ailing one.

How did this happen?

Historically, we have been a centrist nation, tending only slightly to the conservative side of center.

However, since the 1960s, rebellion against authority has become open and acceptable. This arose from a rational disappointment with authority and the loss of confidence in government. There was a time when American society was conservative, traditional and centered on the family. Now, the state has largely replaced the authority and responsibility of the family.

The restrictions of authority serve to keep the middle or secondary layer of the human structure in check. The rapid removal of these checks allows the destructive behavior and ideologies contained in the middle layer to erupt into society.

A dramatic example of what happens with the sudden collapse of authority occurred when the totalitarian Soviet Union folded. When the brutal authority of the Soviets collapsed, the people who had never learned to function from their core were unable to live from their core, and this led to an explosion of criminality, violence, greed and all the other secondary layer activity.

In America, our government, rather than protecting core values, has shifted to the protection of secondary layer function. This gives human destructive behavior free rein and further causes the disintegration of society with increasing crudeness, excessive greed, acting out, political correctness and loss of respect. This adds to confusion and uncertainty and raises general anxiety.

The loss of the authority is seen not only in government and respect for law enforcement, but in respect for the older, more life-experienced segment of society. America is perceived as a young person's country. Senior citizens are sidelined and marginalized. With few exceptions, most authority is openly questioned. Everyone becomes an expert after acquiring a few facts from the Internet. We have difficulty distinguishing between opinion and knowledge.

This shift away from core values also results in:

- Instant gratification instead of waiting for the fruits of your labor

- Distraction from the real issues by TV, media, blogs and all matter of electronic babble

- Rampant greed

- The polarization of society in which left and right become increasingly antagonistic to each other rather than seeking the middle ground, the center, the core.

- A shift in the individual's relationship to society. In the days of the authoritarian society, freedom was somewhat restricted, but there was an emphasis on independence and respect.

- Freedom is replaced by a sense of entitlement, contempt for authority and diminished personal respect.

- Laws, that once were intended to protect core function, become subverted and used for political agendas. The recent federal lawsuit against Arizona's border law and the overturning of Proposition 8 in California in which a judge overturned the will of millions of Californians who voted against the legalization of same-sex marriage are just the most recent examples.

When our founding fathers wrote the Constitution and the Bill of Rights, America was basically a conservative society. They could not have predicted what exists today. They could not have envisioned an

America in which so many people are so removed from their core that they believed the false promises and the propaganda of hope peddlers who promised them a utopia where they were entitled to live off the labors of their fellow man and would be nursed by the state.

This flight away from core values allows the more extreme character types to flourish. As we shall see in the next chapter, the extreme liberal and the extreme conservative, more distant from their core functioning, polarize and split us further from each other.

Chapter 6
Extremes. From Liberal to Communist, From Conservative to Fascist

Convictions are more dangerous enemies of truth than lies.

~ Nietzsche

Extremes are dangerous to our health, whether it's smoking, drinking or politics. Our shift to the left has been so massive that the extreme liberal who was once on the fringe is now regarded as mainstream. On the other side, there's the risk some may move to the extreme right in reaction to the leftward displacement.

There are only two directions to move away from our core. We can move either to the left or to the right as we become more rigid in our views. Usually, the liberal will move further to the left while the conservative more to the right. In moving further away from center the conservative or liberal becomes rigid in his views and more prone to destructive ideas and actions as he loses contact with his core.

Political character types to the left of the liberal include the socialist and ultimately the communist. Conservative character types, if they become more extreme, become reactionary conservatives and eventually fascists.

While most liberals and conservatives start close to the left or right of center, each has the potential to move away and become more rigid and destructive to society as they express their middle layer and lose contact with their core.

Let us briefly look at what happens when a person moves further to the left or to the right. Here, our concept of the three-layered functioning of a person helps us to understand the more extreme characters who populate the political scene.

Shift to the Right

The conservative retains some feeling for his core but the more his core impulses are blocked from expression, the more the energy contained in these frustrated impulses becomes trapped in the middle layer making this middle layer stronger, harsher and more brutal. The frustrations and destructive impulses are usually held in check, but they can become overwhelming and break through into expression. As the conservative moves further to the right, he becomes more rigid, less tolerant of others and more selective of his group. He becomes more fundamentalist in his religion. White supremacists are an extreme example of this tendency. Eventually fascism arises with belief in racial dominance, privilege only for the selected few, and is expressed with harshness, absolute authority and brutality. Examples of this include the Nazi and the Islamic fascist.

Racism rears its ugly head in the shift to the extreme right. The reactionary white conservative has less regard for civil rights while the black reactionary, such as the Black Panther, believes that the white man is inferior. The fascist lies at the extreme right of the spectrum and is extremely rigid, racist, brutal and lives almost completely in his middle layer. He rejects the spontaneity and sexuality of life (he covers up his women) and will go to great lengths to impose order and his will on others.

Shift to the Left

When the liberal character moves further to the left, he becomes an extreme liberal dwelling in the realm of ideas and ideologies. The qualities of the liberal character become exaggerated and more rigid and core contact is eventually lost altogether. He sees government, central control, as the answer to society's problems. Individual responsibility is devalued and ideology becomes more important. Peace is prized more highly more than freedom and liberty. Individual initiative is reduced. Religious feeling is lost and, in the extreme case, the communist replaces religion with ideas and the state replaces God. Justice is by decree, and the Communist regime's imposition of will and collectivization is ruthless. The individual becomes just a tool of the state.

So from this schema, we can see how destructiveness in the political arena increases with the distance from core. It's important to recognize this because what's happening now to our country is a consequence of radicalization and shift to the left in society, in politics and in law. This further movement to the left is often disguised as caring for the individual.

Many liberals, who still retain feelings from their core, become silent partners and eventually active supporters of the extreme liberal who poses as one of them. These healthier liberal characters feel uncomfortable with the extreme movement to the left, but they don't know where else to turn.

To regain our core values, we must avoid an extremist response to this leftward shift. We must stay close to our center and not become extreme and reactionary ourselves. But, just reacting to the shift to the left is not enough. To regain core values requires a definite agenda and plan of action. It requires standing our ground and doing what we believe is right for ourselves and for future generations. Otherwise we might shift too far to the right, away from our core, further polarizing our society.

In order to reestablish balance, we need to know how the radical liberal thinks and operates.

Chapter 7
Why do Liberals Act the Way They Do?

Nearly all men can stand adversity, but if you want to test a man's character, give him power

~Abraham Lincoln

It's much easier to take a person at face value than to examine his character, particularly when we like his smile and want to believe what he says.

Evaluating a person's character is particularly important in politics when the politician masks what he really believes and hides how he sees the world. Occasionally the truth slips out:

Eight more days and I can start telling the truth again

~ Senator Chris Dodd, on the campaign trail

As a rule, a person's character shows itself in the repeated small actions in life. It is more evident under stress, and his character declares itself most openly once he is in a position of power. This principle is clearly evident in that President Obama's character is more obvious since he assumed power. If most independent, centrist voters in this country had realized his character, Barack Obama might not have been elected. It's an old familiar story in politics where the politician presents himself in a way that most attracts popular support and wins opinion.

Those who listened to President Obama's words and did not examine his character are now surprised and disappointed.

We become confused when actions of our leaders don't match their words. Being confused paralyzes an effective response unless we understand why this disconnection between words and actions occurs. We hear people say "I don't understand how the president can support the building of a mosque at the site of 9/11" or "I don't understand why he apologizes to the world for America."

It becomes even harder to understand a person's actions as he become more extreme and alien to the American centrist view.

In this chapter let us examine five aspects of the liberal character that can help us make sense of actions that are otherwise difficult to comprehend:

- Contempt

- Guilt

- Pacifism

- Redistributionism

- Central control

Contempt

The liberal lives largely by means of his intellect. The more extreme liberal, such as President Obama and many members of the current administration are far removed from their core. Their intellect, their braininess, is so prized by themselves and others of like-mind that they look down on those who cannot match their smartness and education. The common man, the working men and women of this country, are viewed with contempt. The intellectual elitism "knows best." But the little slips, the little statements early on in the political campaign that revealed this contempt were ignored and explained away. Barack Obama, while campaigning in Pennsylvania, referred to the little people "clinging to their religion and guns." Not only the President, but others, lecture, talk down to the people they are supposed to lead and represent. It's hard to believe it but they are dripping with contempt. Liberals view conservatives as moronic and stupid. This attitude becomes very clear once you understand the contempt behind it.

Guilt and Pacifism

The more extreme liberal cannot tolerate rational aggression. He wants peace at any price. He sees himself as a world citizen and actually dislikes nationalism, even disdaining his own country and its successes. His expression of concern for the humanitarian needs of other people conceals his contempt and disregard for their welfare and hides his fear of the aggression and force necessary to protect people. Our administration's silence on the brutal suppression of the recent uprising of popular resistance against the Iranian theocracy is an example of this avoidance of any confrontation. Our official response was firstly silence, then empty words but no action.

The "apology tour" in which our president, in the guise of reaching out to the world, of making peace, of making amends, in which he apologized for the exceptionalism and success of America was an embarrassment to those who love their country and a betrayal of those who gave their lives to build and protect the freedoms that spring from this country. Once we see how the extreme liberal views the world, once we see his character, we then have a basis for understanding his actions. He will act similarly in multiple different situations and scenarios because his character is fixed and, unlike ideas, does not change.

The hardwiring that forms the extreme liberal's character does not allow him to recognize the destructive intentions that come from the middle layer of others.

He cannot understand the murderous hate of the terrorist.

In fact the "T" word has been dropped. Janet Napolitano, Homeland Secretary, refused to use the word terrorism and instead referred to "man-made disaster." The extreme liberal desperately tries to whitewash the destructive and evil intentions of fanatics who seek to destroy us.

Redistributionism and Central Control

Everything must be made equal and subject to government control.

America is based on exceptionalism, individual effort and incentive for hard work. Reward for risk-taking and personal responsibility for both success and failure is the essence of the capitalist system. The extreme liberal does not share these values. He disdains the free-market because it requires aggression, and strong will is needed to make your way in the jungle of business and making a living. He sees capitalism as heartless, greedy and cruel. He favors government control over the free market and federal control rather than local. This serves to displace individual responsibility onto the state. The stated motive is to help the underdog, but, in reality, it is to eliminate success and competition. The disparity between the stated intention and the real effects on our economy is becoming more obvious by the day as the free-market is restricted and paralyzed by new rules, regulations and suppression of incentives with increased taxation. Examples of burdensome new regulations and rules contained in the financial reform and health reform acts are too numerous to mention.

The extreme liberal is obsessed with "improvement" and social change. There is usually a sense of urgency to institute these changes.

This sense of urgency often overrides responsibility and clouds good judgment.

In this light, we can begin to see beyond the rhetoric and words. The stated motive, although well intended and truly felt, is seldom the real one, which is best judged by the effects of the actions.

For most of us, the way we see world, ourselves, and our dominant beliefs is acted out on a very small stage. Our opinions and actions affect us personally and the few people closest to us. But the actions of the politician impact the lives of hundreds, thousands or even millions of citizens and, in the case of a world power, countless lives outside the border of his country.

The power vested in a public official, be it a school board member, a town mayor, a congressman or ultimately the President of the United States, carries with it enormous responsibility to uphold our core values as enshrined in the Constitution. Their responsibility is do what they genuinely believe is best for the country and their fellow citizens. If the public official has little core contact, he will act out his personal beliefs and character to mold and change society in whatever way he considers best. His policies and agenda will reflect how close to or how far from core functioning he stands.

That we have entrusted ourselves and our future to the extreme liberal character is becoming all too obvious. Many people are waking up to find they are being pulled too far away from their core values, but they have yet to understand why.

Now that we have a working concept of the liberal character, we can turn to find practical ways to recognize and respond to the extreme liberal's methods and agenda.

Part II

Fighting Back
Reclaiming Our Core Values

Freedom is never more than one generation away from extinction. We didn't pass it to our children in the bloodstream. It must be fought for, protected, and handed on for them to do the same, or one day we will spend our sunset years telling our children and our children's children what it was once like in the United States where men were free.

~ Ronald Reagan

Part II of *Core Values* helps us to use our core feelings and knowledge of character to resist those who undermine our core values.

CHAPTER 8
RESPONDING TO ATTACKS FROM THE LEFT

Public opinion in this country is everything.

~ Abraham Lincoln

We need to know the extreme liberal's motives and tactics because his attacks are sharp, corrosive, and often very personal. His strategy is to control opinion, which Webster's dictionary defines as "belief stronger than impression and less strong than positive knowledge."

There are many ways to suppress a person's freedom. You can put him in prison where it doesn't matter what he thinks because he is shut off from society. Barring that possibility, you can go after his core beliefs.

Here's how it works. The extreme liberal urgently wants to shape the world the way he thinks it ought to be. The core-functioning, freedom-loving individual stands in his way. The only way the extreme liberal can neutralize our opposition is to attack our core or to separate us from our core feelings and values. Once he successfully does so, we are no longer anchored in our core values. When our core feelings become dim and distant, once our heads are filled with conflicting and swirling ideas, we become vulnerable and open to accepting the extreme liberal's opinions as true and, ultimately, as our own. Then he can replace our core values with his ideas and ideology.

This is the principle behind the extreme liberal's campaign to control our opinions. There is no other reason to control somebody else's opinion other than to enforce your agenda. To control somebody else's opinion is an anti-core function because it goes against the core impulse to live and let live, to respect individuality and to uphold individual life in another person. Wanting to control another person is the antithesis of loving your neighbor as yourself.

I realize I'm expressing these principles in a very blunt and direct way, but I feel strongly about the attacks against our right to live from our core. I resent any attempt to weaken us. I don't like to think of people as being so destructive and nasty, but it's true. Just look around and see the negative results when people give up their strength and look outside themselves for salvation.

The battle to change our opinion is more than a sales pitch to get our votes although that's the first step. The destructive effects of the extreme liberal's policies extend beyond his assumption of power. He aims to reshape society by replacing core functions and values with ideologies that impoverish those it was supposed to help.

With these principies in mind, this chapter lists ways the extreme liberal tries to get us to accept his ideas, to empower him and ultimately convince us to give up our freedom for what he puts forth as the "common good". His methods include:

1. Personal attacks
2. Media abuse
3. Motives disguised as good intentions
4. Crisis abuse
5. Contempt
6. Entitlement
7. Political correctness
8. Peddling hope
9. Justice in lieu of freedom
10. Guilt
11. Victimhood

I have broken down each of these into *red flags*, *real reasons* and *response*.

The *red flags* are the feelings that arise from our core to warn us that we are threatened or are deviating from our core values. These feelings are a sixth sense, a gut feeling that tells us that something is wrong.

The *real reasons* are what motivate the extreme liberal's actions.

The *response* is a personal life-positive course of action. It prevents the reflex or knee-jerk reaction that the life-negative action would otherwise provoke. In each instance it is a two-step process in which we think before we act:

PERCEIVE

- Acknowledge our core response (feelings that something is wrong)

- Then ask: Is this life positive? What's the intention? What are the expected results? What is he really saying and how does he expect me to respond? Can I see any core values in this?

ACT

- Engage the threat, protect our core and values or

- Disengage, remove ourselves from the toxicity, then

- Test our response by affirming our core values

This is a general guide to responding to the warnings from our core by comparing everything to our values and acting accordingly. Let us now look at specific instances.

1. Personal Attacks

The further an opinion is from the core, the more aggressively it has to be defended against truth. The defender of the weaker opinion feels threatened and acts like a cornered animal. He engages the life-negative impulses from his secondary layer as he goes on the offense using whatever means he can to resist truth. This explains why personal attacks spew forth a mixture of hate, nastiness in defense of a position.

As we move further from center, there is less true debate and exchange of knowledge. There is a battle to control and justify each opinion. The more extreme the battle for our opinion, the shriller and nastier the attack and defense of the opinion becomes.

This is an important guidepost: expressions of hate and personal attacks to defend one's position are a significant departure from core values.

Truth speaks with a quiet firm voice which can be drowned out by the barrage of verbiage and personal opinion.

Red Flag: When our person, and not just our opinion, is attacked, often sarcastically and with contempt, our core reacts to the perceived danger with feelings of anger, fear or sometimes both. By contrast, a genuine exchange of opinion does not engage our core because it is not threatening.

Real Reason: The real reason for going after us personally is the attacker's fear of being exposed. The attack is based on the principle that attack is the best form of defense. Making the attack personal is designed to make us feel threatened and force us to retreat from our position.

Response: We hold true to our values. We look for the real reason for the attack as we defend our position and integrity.

PERCEIVE

- I feel that am being attacked. How does he expect me to respond to this nasty attack? Does he expect

44

me to fold and to retreat or is he baiting me? Is there anything of core value here?

ACT

- I choose to *engage*. I stand up and expose the reasons behind this attack. Why are you accusing me or attacking me? You're doing so to avoid truth and honest discussion. You are wrong and here's the truth.

- I *disengage* if I feel there is nothing to be gained in engaging this person. I walk away, I turn my back.

- I affirm that my truth and center is solid and untouchable. I remind myself that nothing can enter my being that defiles or makes a lie unless I allow it to do so.

The charge of racism, when used in the battle for opinion, is an example of the personal attack. Calling a person a racist is designed to make him defensive and to distract attention away from the real core issues. It's a serious and nasty tactic which draws on the collective guilt of the past and dumps it on the individual. The charge of racism to attack opposing opinion is a sure indicator of the weakness of the liberal's position.

Those of us who treasure core values are colorblind. We are all individual manifestations of the same life source. We prize character. We look at the policies not the melanin content of the skin.

The liberal has an army of help to promote his views– the media.

2. Media Abuse

Half a truth is often a great lie.

~Benjamin Franklin

The media is largely populated by liberal characters (just as, by contrast, the military, and law enforcement tend to attract people of a conservative character). Because the liberal lives largely in his head, he is attracted to careers in the media, academia and journalism. The liberal expresses his opinions well. The more extreme liberals are writers of opinion articles in magazines and, with few exceptions, television is slanted to the left because of the filtering effect of character.

The media has largely become the mouthpiece for the liberal agenda. Stories that bolster the liberal image are reported while others are minimized or ignored altogether.

Disinformation and expression of shrill opinions come directly from the secondary layer.

The nasty and hateful personal attacks against George Bush, Sarah Palin, or anyone else who openly expresses conservative views pervades the media. The hate and contempt is very ugly. Journalists, who were once able to suppress their emotions in order to report the truth, no longer do so.

The Internet is also a powerful instrument for disseminating propaganda. The Internet allows anyone who can type to put forward his opinion creating a dust storm of opinions and banality. In this "blogosphere" it becomes very difficult to sort out knowledge from opinion. The absence of face-to-face or personal contact on the Internet encourages cowardly and personal attacks.

Red Flag: We feel uneasy when the media selectively reports facts to serve a particular viewpoint. This is because there is a mismatch between what is reported and what we feel to be true. In a way we are being asked to move away from our center to accept somebody else's truth. We feel even more uneasy when such media launches personal attacks and expresses contempt for other opinions.

Real Reason: The goal is to control our opinion by distorting the facts.

Response:

PERCEIVE

- Is the reporting direct, open and honest? Is the reporting devious? Why don't I trust this reporting?

- Here are some good questions to ask when watching, reading or listening to the media: Is this true? What's their purpose in reporting this? Do I feel uneasy because of the facts or because of the way it is reported? If so, why do I feel uneasy? Is the reporting direct, open and honest or is it devious? Why don't I trust this TV personality?

ACT

- I choose to *engage* by obtaining my facts from A variety of sources while, at the same time, keeping an open mind. Once I've checked the facts, I will find a way to speak the truth to others, particularly when they regurgitate the undigested media feed.

- I *disengage* by switching off the television, changing channels and turning to more positive pursuits.

- I affirm that I have to think for myself and test everything I read, see on television or on the Internet against my core values

As an aside, excessive television watching sedates the critical and analytic part of our brain making us more likely to accept what we see on the tube as fact.

Truth is drowned out in the shrill defense of ideology. Remember, as Abraham Lincoln well knew, the battle is for the control of our opinion.

Opinion can be confused with knowledge, and we have to test each opinion we are exposed to against our core values.

3. Motives Disguised as Good Intentions

Trying to appreciate the true motives behind a statement or opinion is a challenge in daily life and is most difficult in politics.

The extreme liberal so believes in the good intentions of his actions that he is blind to the negative or destructive effects of his ideas. His dishonesty may not be conscious but a shortsightedness or refusal to look ahead and evaluate the outcome of his policies. His drive to enact his ideals on the social scene is so strong and is done with such urgency that he overlooks the practical and long-term effects of his policies. Because his ideals come from his head and not from his core, the effects of well-intentioned policies can be nearly disastrous. The housing crisis is an example. There are many factors involved, but the well-meaning intention of encouraging home ownership for people who could not afford their loans triggered the mortgage crisis.

Red Flag: Something inside makes us feel uncomfortable when stated intentions sound too good to be true. This discomfort, creeping doubt or cynicism are signals to "watch out." Again the mismatch between words and the feelings from our core produces an inner tension that makes us feel uneasy.

Real Reason: Hiding one's motives by saying one thing but meaning another is dishonest. It is a trick to circumvent open dialogue, to avoid transparency and bypass resistance.

The health-care bill is a good example of this sleight-of-hand. The stated motives for reforming healthcare are good and altruistic. To be sure, our health-delivery system is not perfect and needs improvement. However, the effects of The Patient Protection and Affordable Health Care Act (PPACA) are not as transparent as the stated intention. The creation of 150 new federal bureaucracies hides the real agenda which is to expand government control of the individual. We are slowly waking up to the dishonesty and deception as our core values are bypassed in the name of the common good.

Response: We have to look at the effect, the fruit, of the action and not the words. We predict, as best we can, what we think the outcome will be and then compare that, not the words, against our core values.

    PERCEIVE

- What is the reason for my feeling of unease? What's wrong with this good sounding idea? Is there a hidden agenda behind it? What will be the result and outcome of this intended plan or policy? Will the effect strengthen me as an individual and uphold my freedom? Or will the end result strip me away from my core and dilute my core values?

    ACT

- I choose to *engage* and confront the possible dishonesty. I will turn to trusted sources such as the

Heritage Foundation for analysis of complex issues, and I will support such organizations in whatever way I can. Then, I will speak out to reveal the hidden motives and help others to see the truth. At least, I will express my doubts so that they may think it out for themselves and not accept the good intentions at face value.

- *Disengagement* is not an option because this is exactly the intended effect of hidden motives which is to bypass my resistance.

- I affirm my core value of having truth revealed openly and directly. Anything else is suspect.

4. Panic and Alarm

Almost every agenda from the Obama administration is "urgent" or "critical" as we are asked to act quickly before things get worse. Whether it's the financial bailouts, healthcare, Gulf oil spill, or carbon dioxide in the atmosphere, the situation is always dire. Those who seek to advance their political and social agenda exploit our vulnerability rather than responding to the crisis by stabilizing then rationally and transparently examining the options.

During a crisis we feel vulnerable, confused and anxious and look to government for stability and help.

The synergism between the extreme liberal agenda and the media is revealed during a crisis as the media fans the flames of any crisis often making it larger than it is. By doing so, the media promotes the extreme liberal's subterfuge in using a crisis to push through his political agenda. A glaring example is using the largely manufactured global warming crisis as a reason to push Cap and Trade legislation and to give a government agency (Environmental Protection Agency) greater control over our personal lives.

Red Flag: One crisis on top of another adds to our feeling of vulnerability and helplessness. When there are too many predictions of doom and calamity, when everything is urgent and needs to be fixed NOW, we suspect our government's motives because we are being asked to override our innate caution. A scenario of impending disaster lends urgency to fix healthcare, global warming, finances and international situations. We feel uncomfortable because this urgency does not allow us time to think things through. We feel a spontaneous sense of resistance to being railroaded into something we are not ready for. More than ever, during a crisis, we need to stay in contact with our core feelings.

Real Reason: The extreme liberal is anxious to push his agenda and needs to rush everything.

A sense of crisis allays the extreme liberal's anxiety because it provides him with an opportunity to rapidly change society the way he thinks it ought to be. He creates a sense of such urgency so as to override our core response and to make us feel confused, helpless so that we turn to our leaders for guidance during yet another crisis.

Response:

PERCEIVE

- I follow my feelings of doubt and resistance to being pushed into something that doesn't feel right.

- With any crisis, we stop, take a deep breath and ask:

  How bad is the crisis? Is this crisis being exploited to move me further away or closer to my core values?

Why don't I trust them? Is the response to the crisis one of preserving and protecting our freedom, security, and future? Is this crisis being used in any way to further an ideological political agenda? If so, will the result support or negate my core values?

ACT

- *Engage*: I will do what I can to help those affected by this crisis. Perhaps I will donate to the Red Cross or a relief agency if the crisis is a natural disaster. I will support government efforts if they are constructive and support life and freedom. But, I will express my concern and doubt about hidden agendas if I sense that a crisis is being manipulated for political ends.

- *Disengage*: Standing back and doing nothing is not an option because it fuels my sense of helplessness, which is exactly what the manipulators want. If I feel unable to help as an individual, I can lend my support and presence to a group of like-minded people.

- I affirm that our core values will guide us in the right direction to coping with and solving each crisis. I reject any response that goes contrary to life and liberty.

In summary, the components of crisis abuse include:

1. Exploiting a crisis for pushing forward a political and social agenda.

2. Injecting a sense of excessive urgency to create confusion and anxiety. Was healthcare so urgent? The only real urgency,

the only real crisis was to push a social agenda which prevented debate and transparency.

But we have to pass the bill so that you can find out what is in it.

~ Nancy Pelosi

This is not how democracy works. It is how regimes operate! Many of our representatives in Washington caved in to the pressure created by the hyped up sense of urgency. Their abdication of responsibility shows how far they are from core values and how distant they are from the interests of the people they represent.

5. Contempt

When those in power talk down or lecture to us, we are made to feel inferior. It's like being back in school and listening to the teacher. A sense of intellectual superiority is often expressed as contempt for those who don't agree with them.

Red Flag: We feel devalued, personally attacked, and stupid when intellectual superiority bubbles up into open contempt. We feel that we're being demeaned and disparaged, and our core doesn't like that. We feel the same response as when we are personally attacked. Our core-response to this is to say "no!" You have it wrong. We also express this feeling by referring to the intellectuals as "cold", or "removed" from us.

Real Reason: The extreme liberal tends to use his well-developed intellect as a weapon. His opponent, the conservative, is often cast as a buffoon, a moron and stupid. Think of how the left categorizes Ronald Reagan, Bush and other conservatives.

Mental sharpness is healthy as long as the brain is used to express core feelings. But, when someone's intellect is used to override or go against feelings that come from his core, his thinking can become life-defeating rather than life-ennobling.

Response: Once we recognize that someone is using their mind as a weapon, we recognize the attack method for what it and return to our core values to regain our confidence.

PERCEIVE

- I follow the feeling of being demeaned and ask:

Why is he trying to make me feel stupid? Am I really that dumb? What does he hope to achieve by talking down to me? How does he expect me to react? Do his actions express any core values?

ACT

- I *engage* by bringing this person's attention to the fact that he's talking down to me, and I will ask him why he is doing so.

- I *disengage*. I can choose to ignore this form of personal attack if I feel that he is baiting me and trying to draw me into a clever debate in order to show off his intellect and education.

- I affirm my own worth and will not allow this person to make me doubt myself. I recognize that his actions do not arise from his core because they don't respect another's life.

6. Entitlement

Almost 47% of Americans pay no federal income tax yet they receive the benefits that flow from citizenship. More and more people are rendered helpless and look to the government to take care of them.

Red Flag: We feel a creeping despair in response to anything that reduces our incentive to be creative, to take risks and to be responsible for our efforts. We feel robbed by laws that entitle others to live off our work. We become angry at the growing sense of entitlement, of reward without effort, not only because it contravenes our core values but because we instinctively dislike anything that weakens us by devitalizing our core.

Real Reason: Under the guise of supporting and caring for those less fortunate (which, in itself, is a core function) the liberal in power claims to know best and will confiscate the fruits of our hard work to give it to those he thinks needs or deserves support. Charitable giving, a core function, is taken from the individual and replaced by state policy. This gives central government greater power and more control over the people. The extreme liberal is empowered when the helpless and weakened masses turn to him for help and salvation thus giving him the opportunity to redistribute wealth and enact his ideas.

Response:

PERCEIVE

- I follow the dual feelings of frustration and anger.

- I ask: Why do I feel that the sense of entitlement to so unfair? Are these programs helping or hurting people? What's the real intention of making them feel entitled to government handouts? Is it fair that I support them in addition to supporting my family and community? What is the difference between helping someone in need and making them feel entitled to that help? I encourage my children to be strong and independent, so why doesn't the government to the same for its children?

ACT

- *Engage:* My response is strong and direct as I affirm my core values. I have the right to honest and fulfilling work, and I accept responsibility for the rewards and risks of my work. Everyone else, who is able to do so, should do the same. I willingly give a portion of my earnings to those I choose to help.

- *Disengage*: Not responding is not an option because passivity and silence not only fuels the entitlement but puts me at risk for thinking that I'm also entitled to the fruit of another's work.

7. Changing the Meaning of Words - Political Correctness

The culture of political correctness results from the shift of society to the left, away from core. This movement away from core values provides the fertile soil for the extreme liberal to control our opinions and to enact his social ideas. One way to do this is to stifle and dilute truth by altering the meaning of words.

Expression of truth from the core is always respectful, direct and honest.

Political correctness is its opposite because it strips truth from the word. The author Doris Lessing has this insight:

Political correctness is the natural continuum from the party line. What we are seeing once again is a self-appointed group of vigilantes imposing their views on others. It is a heritage of communism, but they don't seem to see this.

Red Flag: We feel like we're being strangled when we have to stifle our true thoughts. Changing words to more acceptable terms makes us feel that we can no longer speak the truth, or at least that we will be judged harshly by speaking the truth. This frustrates us. The further away from truth, the more distorted the meanings of words become, and we begin to feel that familiar discomfort as our core cautions us not to stray too far from our center and truth.

Real Reason: Political correctness is the modern morality. It functions to obscure truth. Political correctness is no more complicated than that. Political correctness also is a way to level the playing field and to make society equal by force of morals. This moralistic attitude to controlling what we express is the precursor to state-enforced control of what we can say. For example, I'm a "health-care provider" and no longer a physician, neurologist or a doctor. The generic term serves the socialist ideal of bringing everyone down to same level.

Response:

PERCEIVE

- I recognize political correctness for what it is.

- I ask: Why can't I directly express what I know to be true? What will happen if I do so? Who says that I have to avoid truth? Why can't we call a terrorist a terrorist? What's the effect of changing the words, and why does the government lead the way to changing words? Is political correctness dishonest? Am I really protecting the feeling of others by using watered-down words? Is there any core value in using politically correct terms?

ACT

- *Engage*: I cannot change the culture of political correctness, but I will reinterpret the altered words and recognize the deviation from truth. Asking somebody what they mean when they use a politically correct term may help that person realize what they are doing.

- *Disengage*: I don't have to change the minds of others. I don't have to throw the meaning of the word back in the person's face and become confrontational.

- I select whether to engage or disengage by asking whether the effects of engaging another person are a life positive response from my core or am I reacting out of anger.

- I affirm the inherent truthfulness of my core and will not allow anybody to remove me from what I know to be true.

8. Peddling Hope and Empty Promises

President Obama was elected on a wave of optimism fed by his promises of change and hope. We all desire freedom and happiness and naturally look to a leader who promises us a chicken in every pot. A person who promises hope and happiness for nothing is a freedom peddler.

Red Flag: It doesn't make sense to us when somebody promises us something in return for nothing. We know that happiness and success are earned. When someone else offers to provide them for us, we feel we are being asked to weaken ourselves, to give up our core to him in exchange for happiness. It doesn't make sense because we know that happiness originates from within us.

Real Reason: The real purpose of the freedom peddler is to weaken our individuality, to remove us from our core by getting us to entrust our lives to him.

Response:

PERCEIVE

- I follow the anger, even feelings of rage, when I see someone exploiting another's misery and weakness.

- I ask: Why am I being asked to believe that this person and his government will make me happy and provide for me? Will it make me stronger or weaker if I trust him? In matters of faith, I look to my minister, priest or rabbi for guidance but I don't expect them to provide my happiness. Why then would I accept these promises from a stranger who may eventually ask me to drink the Kool-Aid in return for what he offers?

ACT

- *Engage.* I resist the temptation to accept enticing promises. I will speak out against hope peddlers. When someone turns his gaze to the government for his happiness, I'll do what I can, gently, lovingly to remind him that his happiness is found within himself.

- *Disengage.* I realize that there are those who are lost and who have given up their souls to someone outside themselves or to the government. There is nothing I can do to change them, as painful as it may be to see it.

- I affirm that true happiness and hope spring from my soul. The Lord is my shepherd – not the government.

9. Justice in the Name of Freedom

The liberal character values justice over liberty and freedom. Anti-core actions are often covered in a sugarcoating of professed concern for individual rights. We feel angry when terrorists are given the full protection of the law while they continue to pose a threat to our life and liberty.

The extreme liberal is sincere in his beliefs because he is unable to distinguish destructive hate-driven acts that arise from the secondary layer from natural-protective aggression that comes from the core.

Red Flag: We feel the impulse to protect our core when we are threatened. We feel a rising anger when we are expected to set aside our protective instincts in the name of justice or some other cause. It doesn't make sense to us when we are asked to expose ourselves to danger and go against our most basic core impulse to love and protect life.

Real Reason: These sugar-coated destructive actions covertly undermine our strength and express the extreme liberal's hidden disdain for his country. His disdain is wrapped up in his intolerance of aggression and his inability to recognize and acknowledge the ugly, hate-laden secondary layer in others.

Response:

PERCEIVE

- I follow the feelings that come from being exposed to danger.

- Then I ask: What is the real purpose of putting a confessed terrorist on trial? What is the effect of doing so? Do I believe that affording these people full civil rights will change them? Am I prepare to accept the consequences of the terrorist being free to kill again? Does this action protect my core or does it serve the destructive middle layer? Am I being asked to place my life in jeopardy in the name of justice?

ACT

- *Engage:* I will speak out to protect family, country and myself. I will call my political representatives. I will join with others who share some other feelings. I will try to expose the hidden motives behind these actions and remind others that we are at war with a relentless and ruthless enemy.

- *Disengage:* this is not an option when our core and country are threatened.

- I affirm that I will do whatever I can to protect the life and freedom of those I love and my country even when those sworn to uphold the Constitution fail to do so.

10. Guilt

The guilt the extreme liberal feels for his success underlies his desire to equalize society. His guilt, which is to be shared by others, is rationalized as tolerance, as understanding his fellow man even those whose behavior, such as criminals, terrorists, is destructive. He believes that no one person should be better or worse than another. Therefore the only solution is to equalize everyone to the lowest common denominator.

Red Flag: We feel uneasy when we are expected to feel guilty for things we have no control over, such as our history of slavery in the past. We feel a rise of protective anger when we are supposed to feel guilty for punishing those who are destructive to life and when we are expected to eschew our core values to suppress any natural aggression. Dumping guilt on us is a very potent weapon because it activates the guilt that most of us do have about certain things in our past.

Real Reason: Guilt makes us feel confused, and it paralyzes our opposition and rational response to the extreme liberal and socialist agenda. In short, we're asked to do more than tolerate destructive behavior, we are expected to atone for our attitude

Response:

PERCEIVE

- I follow the uneasy and protective anger that come from my belly.

- Then I stop and ask: Why am I supposed to feel guilty? What's the purpose of trying to make me feel guilty? Does guilt make me a better person or a weaker one?

Is there any core value in feeling guilty for things that were not my decision? Is guilt a means of attacking me? Is it an attempt to weaken me?

ACT

- *Engage.* I will do whatever I can to act in a life-enhancing way, but I will not atone for the sins of others. I will point out to those around me the ploy behind laying guilt on us.

- *Disengagement* is an option to avoid confrontation with a toxic person who uses whatever tricks he can to draw me into a no-win exchange.

- I affirm that I will only feel guilty if I have contravened my own core values of love and respect for life and my commitment to protect core values of those who are vulnerable. I will not be manipulated into taking ownership of someone else's guilt.

11. Victimhood

A victim is a person who suffers from a hurt or injury inflicted by another. Casting people as victims engenders a culture of victimhood. Victimhood is one step beyond entitlement and guilt. Not only does the "victim" fail to assume responsibility for his shortcomings, he blames others for his situation. It adds revenge and anger to the mix which fuel the sense of righting wrongs.

Red Flag: Every core feeling we have in response to entitlement and guilt is amplified by the culture of victimhood. These feelings include unease and anger at the sense of entitlement.

Real Reason: Encouraging a person or group to feel victimized does several things.

> 1. While ostensibly appealing to a sense of fairness, it encourages people to turn to their leaders and the Government to exact the revenge they feel they deserve.
>
> 2. It fuels a sense of entitlement
>
> 3. It further weakens the individual by displacing him from his core
>
> 4. It dumps guilt onto the person, group or political opposition in order to weaken and paralyze them.
>
> 5. It encourages division, not unity. The Obama administration has promoted the culture of victimhood as part of their plan to divide the nation. Their methods include racial division by evoking a sense of victimhood from the past history of slavery. They also encourage us to feel victimized by the greedy capitalists. This engenders a sense of helplessness. It makes us turn to the Government not only for support but also for revenge against the offending agent thereby giving further energy and power to the extreme liberal's agenda.

Response:

PERCEIVE

- My perception depends on whether I am cast as a victim or am supposed to feel sympathy for the victims.

- If I'm tempted to see myself as a victim I may feel angry because I want to right the wrongs. Then I ask: Am I justified in feeling such anger? What am I really a victim of? How does it help me if I accept that I'm a victim? Am I being asked to identify with others in the group to confirm that we all victims?

- If I stand apart from the victim I then ask: Am I supposed to feel guilty about not helping the victims? Am I part of the problem? Who is the victim of what?

ACT

- *Engage:* I will do what I can to help the true victim who is hurt by the destructiveness of others or by natural disaster. For example I can donate to the Red Cross or offer my physical help and skills.

- *Disengage:* I will not promote the sense of victimhood which strips a person away from his core and empowers those who promote this culture. In this case, I will speak what I know to be true and will avoid the paralyzing trap of guilt.

. . . .

There are also forces that can pull us the other way, to the right, of our core.

CHAPTER 9
RESPONDING TO ATTACKS FROM THE RIGHT

Movement to the extremes in either direction from the core can be equally destructive. The potential destructiveness depends on how far away from core we are, not just whether we have moved to the left or the right.

At the present time we are not much at risk from an extreme right shift because our society has moved so far to the left.

Any rightward or conservative reaction will tend to bring us back towards our center. But it's good to be aware that there's a risk of over-shooting, a swing too far to the right. I will not devote much to that in this chapter because the danger from the right in this country is relatively mild except for the extreme right wing Islamic fascists who are discussed in the next chapter.

Here are some methods used by extreme right-wing or ultra-conservative to accomplish their goals:

1. False piety
2. Sects
3. Racism
4. Ultra-nationalism
5. Automatic allegiance

1. False Piety

True religious feeling arises from our core in acknowledgment of a power greater than our self. I t is not a core function for someone to use his religion to empower himself and to control others.

Red Flag: We feel a sense of mistrust for someone who uses his morality and image of holiness to cover up something else. We become angry when we sense that a posture of holiness is not genuine. The Imams of Islam who preach and condone violence are blatantly using their piety to control others.

Real Reason: The mask of false piety hides the destructive impulses from the secondary layer. Religion can be abused to wield power.

Response:

PERCEIVE

- I follow my sense of mistrust and ask: Why don't I trust him? Is he motivated by tolerance, love and kindness or is he trying to manipulate and control me? Does he practice what he preaches? Does he have any hidden motive for appearing so holy? How does he expect me to respond? Do I see any core values here? What is he hiding?

ACT

- *Engage*: I will speak out and express my doubts if I feel this person is trying to influence the beliefs of others.

- *Disengage*: I turn away, leaving him to his ego, if I sense no hidden agenda here or if his destructive potential is very limited.

- I affirm my own core belief that religious feeling is genuine, natural and never paraded. I recall that Jesus was a carpenter and that Rabbi Hillel supported himself as a woodcutter.

2. Sects

The extreme conservative separates himself from others by becoming elitist. He overvalues his individuality by extending it to a selected group of individuals. Although the healthy conservative values the individual, this can be taken to extremes by favoring some over others. The Tea Party is not a sect because like-minded people gather for a common cause while adhering to core values of individual liberty and respect for the individual.

Red Flag: We feel uneasy and a sense of caution because no one group has a monopoly on truth. Overvaluing the group devalues our own individuality. This is not a core function. The red flag is that we are asked to give up our individuality in order to belong to a select group.

Real Reason: Elitism excludes those who do not share the same ideology. Identifying with a sect provides a false sense of superiority of one individual over another. Whatever the means and methods, devaluing an individual is the antithesis of core function.

Response:

PERCEIVE

- I follow my feeling of caution and inquire: Is my individuality at risk if I join this group? What's the purpose of these people? Does this group function from and promote core values or not? Am I being asked to give up myself to the group?

ACT

- I will *engage* if I sense this group's purpose is destructive. I will then speak out and express my resistance if people are being exploited and are being drawn in to surrender their uniqueness.

- I will *disengage* if I sense this group is a laager, a circling the wagons that offers refuge and a sense of belonging to those who feel vulnerable. I will let them be. Each person can make his own decisions, but I cannot be silent if I sense destructive intent.

- I affirm my right to associate with whom I want. I weigh all my decisions against my core values.

3. Racial Ideology

Ideas of racial purity serve to devalue others, and, like sects, provide a false sense of superiority of one group over another.

Red Flag: Talk of racial purity is repulsive to us because it judges on superficial differences and ignores the core, the center of life in each individual. The identification of individuals as worthy, superior to others based on race, is different from the baseless charges of racism which the liberal uses to personally attack an opposing view. Racial purity was central to Nazism, and a race of true believers is a tenet of Islamic fascists. While racism in America is largely equated with elitism of the whites, we should be aware that extreme right-wing racial ideology is also espoused by the Black Panther movement.

Real Reason: The real reason for racial ideology is to devalue and control us as individuals by forming a select group. This sets the stage for unleashing the accumulated hate and venom of the secondary layer onto other racial and ethnic groups.

Response:

PERCEIVE

- Our strong feelings of revulsion and anger lead us to ask: Why do they want to make themselves superior? What is the result of their actions? Is this racial ideology part of a bigger agenda? How destructive is it?

ACT

- I *engage* because I cannot remain silent here. It is not just the sense of superiority that bothers me but the dangerous gathering storm of hate and destructiveness fueled by such ideology. I will speak out and try to expose this ideology when its spills over into society. I will watch for the spread of this infection because it can be very contagious to others who are tempted to be drawn in.

- I *disengage* if I judge that the degree of destructiveness and receptivity to the ideology is minimal. If this weak idea has not landed in any fertile soil in our society, it will dissolve in its own lie. In such circumstances I will not be drawn into exchanges and fuel it by my reaction.

- I affirm that my core values are colorblind and that the soul has no pigment. I understand the intent of racial ideology and will see it for the lie that it is. It doesn't matter what group claims superiority, talk of racial purity is always an anti-core function.

4. Ultra-nationalism

Extreme nationalism, an anti-core function, is different from patriotism. Patriotism is the natural love of country. Ultra-nationalism is an over-identification with a group to the exclusion of others. It is interesting to note how the extreme characters on the left and on the right begin to resemble each other the further they are away from the core. Jonah Goldberg discusses this aspect in detail in his book *Liberal Fascism*.

The risk of ultra-nationalism in America is minimal because we are such a diverse group of strong individuals.

Red Flag: Ultra-nationalism makes us feel uneasy because it serves the destructive aspect of human character. Our discomfort is the same feeling that we have with a sect, but it is now taken to a national level.

Real Reason: Ultra-nationalism is an extreme reaction to preserve identity by replacing the individual with the state. Extreme nationalism devalues the individual who becomes a servant of the state.

Response:

PERCEIVE

- I follow my discomfort and inquire: What is the intention of being so vigorously nationalistic? How am I expected to respond to this? Are others trying to confuse my natural love of country with the requirement to surrender my individuality to the interests of the state? Is the purpose of this nationalism to impose our collective will on others?

ACT

- I *engage* if I sense a growing movement towards ultra-nationalism and if I sense any destructive potential here. I need to assert my individuality and express my understanding of true patriotism to help others to see the difference between patriotism and extreme identification with a group.

- I *disengage* if talk of extreme nationalism is local and if it has little following. I will ignore it if it is just talk without destructive power.

- I affirm my own core values of love of country and respect for the individual, whoever he is and wherever he lives.

5. Automatic Allegiance to a Leader

The further a leader moves from the core the more authoritarian he becomes, the less dissent he will tolerate and the more he expects unquestioning obedience from his followers. As we have noted, the functions of the communist dictator and of the fascist dictator are very similar. Only their methods and uniforms differ. An extreme example of automatic allegiance to a leader is the cult of leader-worship in communist North Korea.

Red Flag: We are repelled by anyone who expects us to surrender our individual choice and freedom.

Real Reason: The motive is to obtain power and control over others by stripping them from their core.

Response:

PERCEIVE

- My strong feeling of protective anger leads me to ask these questions before I react: What is he asking me to do? What will result if I see him as my leader? Do I sense anything of core value here? Do I trust him?

- I recognize the unquestioning obedience to the leader as part of a cult.

ACT

- I'll *engage* by resisting, speaking out and asserting my individuality to protect my freedom if I feel any pressure to follow someone blindly or if I sense he is trying to separate me from my core.

- I may *disengage* if it is a local egotist whose destructive potential is contained and limited. I can walk away leaving each person to make up his own mind.

- I affirm that I will never surrender my freedom and individuality.

It does not matter to our core what direction we move, the only thing that matters is if we are being pulled away from it.

The protective impulses and feelings that arise from our core are the same whether we respond to the extreme right or to the extreme left. The difference between the extreme left and extreme right lies in the ideology and methods that each uses to make us surrender our core values.

CHAPTER 10
UNWITTING FRIENDS OF OUR ENEMIES - THE DANGER FROM WITHIN

Liberals, it has been said, are generous with other peoples' money, except when it comes to questions of national survival when they prefer to be generous with other people's freedom and security.

~ William F. Buckley, Jr.

Following the brutal attacks of September 11, 2001, our country shifted back to center on a surge of protective conservative reaction. We returned to our core values as we came together to deal with tragedy and to confront our enemy. This unity of purpose, unfortunately, didn't last long. As the long-standing divisions in our country reappeared, our unanimity cracked apart, and we moved even further to the left of core than before September 11. In the face of a persistent fanatical enemy, instead of being strengthened in a common defense, we are being weakened and exposed by the extreme liberal characters in power. As a nation, we ignored character and elected a pacifist commander-in-chief in a time of war.

Our slide away from center has reached such a degree that we now support the building of a mosque on the site of the first major Islamic-fascist attack on our homeland. Not only are we being dragged away from respect for those brave souls who died in the tragedy, but such an action signals our weakness to our enemies. All this is done in the name of peace, tolerance and understanding.

This is America. And our commitment to religious freedom must be unshakeable. The principle that people of all faiths are welcome in this country and that they will not be treated differently by their government is essential to who we are...And that includes the right to build a place of worship and a community center on private property in Lower Manhattan, in accordance with local laws and ordinances.

~ Barack Obama

The debate about this mosque reveals the characters involved and their respect for or negation of core values.

(Obama) has abandoned America at the place where America's heart was broken nine years ago, and where her true values were on display for all to see. Now this president declares that the victims of 9/11 and their families must bear another burden. We must stand silent at the last place in America where 9/11 is still remembered with reverence or risk being called religious bigots.

~ 9/11 Families for a Safe & Strong America

To see how far to the left our country has drifted over the years, consider what our response would have been after World War II if the Japanese had wanted to build a Shinto shrine at Pearl Harbor.

Our nation is at war with Islamo-fascists who will kill as many Americans as they can and who aim to destroy our society. Some pundits have called this world war IV (the Cold War being World War III), and this is a very different war to any other in history. It will be a long protracted struggle against fanatics who place no value on any life, including their own. To prevail, we have to understand the enemy because he uses any means to exploit and weaken us. The Islamic fanatic's aims have been openly stated, and he will exploit any cracks or weaknesses in our strength.

I won't dwell on theories about why Islamic jihadist fanatics hate America and want to destroy us. Their brutality is a given, especially after the attacks of September 11, 2001. Numerous theories abound to explain the origins of this hate and terrorism, but there can be no doubt that these fanatics hate us and will seek out every in every way to harm us. The majority of Muslims remain silent, giving a quiet acquiescence to the extremists.

Given the indisputable fact that the Islamic jihadist's agenda is to destroy us, why then are we exposing our belly?

The extreme liberal acts as an unwitting ally to the jihadists.

Our enemies see appeasement, talk and no action, conciliatory letters to the Ayatollah and apology speeches in Cairo as signs of our weakness.

Why do the extreme liberals in power and their more moderate liberal supporters act this way? Why don't they see the danger? Perhaps they cannot see it or perhaps they unconsciously hate America?

Red Flags: We have a strong emotional reaction to the list of liberal conciliatory actions: closing of Guantánamo Bay, Miranda rights for terrorists, changing the name of terrorists to "enemy combatants", pushing for civilian trials of confessed bombers. We feel confused when we are told we should understand our enemies and talk nicely to them. Does it mean that we don't understand our enemy? It doesn't make sense. We begin to doubt ourselves. Perhaps some of the terrorists are "nice guys" after all. Do those in power know something we don't? The mismatch between core values and these actions is so huge that we have a hard time believing what we see.

More than ever, we have to understand not only our enemy but those among us who, unwittingly or intentionally, weaken us in the face of an enemy hell-bent on our destruction. We can only do so by knowing the character from which these placatory actions spring. Unless we understand the origins of this self-defeating pacifism, it will never make sense to us, particularly when actions of appeasement are presented as well-intended and humanitarian.

Real Reasons: The liberal, particularly the extreme liberal, as we have seen, has little core contact. He cannot tolerate aggression. Physical aggression is abhorrent to him. He would rather dwell in the realm of concepts and ideals than deal with the ugly reality around him. Not only does he disdain aggression, but he is unable to recognize and acknowledge the destructive intent of others. As he has minimal contact with his core, he cannot sense the hate and destructive impulses contained in the secondary layer of others. He refuses to accept that bad people cannot be transformed into better ones who will respect life if only we understood them.

When we couple this with the liberal's feelings of guilt and his desire for revenge against authority, we have all sorts of subconscious motives that underlie the extreme liberal's policy of exposing us to our enemies. Remember that the extreme liberal's intellect prevents him from feeling the life positive impulses that arise from his core. He can't distinguish between healthy aggression to protect life and the brutal life-killing aggression from the secondary layer. So he avoids both and gives logical reasons for his actions that don't match our core values.

Response: Once we see behind the pacifism, we can understand that arguments, policies and words disguise the intent to weaken us. Not only does the extreme liberal character in power encourage our enemies, he weakens us from within by sapping our strength with his destructive fiscal and social policies.

The current danger to our nation is vastly underestimated. Once we realize the magnitude of the threat, we will hold those in power accountable and seek, by every legitimate means, to replace them with those who function closer to their core. We remind ourselves that aggression from the core is not destructive but serves to protect life and liberty. When we feel angry, we can channel our surge of protective energy constructively to expose the motives and intent of those who weaken us and encourage and support, from within the political and legal process, others who share our core values. Those leaders, who function from their core, will rise only when we the people are ready for them and call them forth.

The Leadership Traits of the Marine Corps.

The Marine Corps manual lists 14 leadership traits. When we compare their 14 leadership traits with those of our current political leaders, the paucity of core values in Washington becomes starkly evident. The 14 leadership traits of the Marines are:

BEARING   Creating a favorable impression in carriage, appearance, and personal conduct at all times.

COURAGE   A mental quality that recognizes fear of danger or criticism, but enables a Marine to proceed in the face of it with calmness and firmness.

DECISIVENESS   Ability to make decisions promptly and to announce them in a clear, forceful manner.

DEPENDABILITY   The certainty of proper performance of duty.

ENDURANCE   The mental and physical stamina measured by the ability to withstand pain, fatigue, stress, and hardship.

ENTHUSIASM   The display of sincere interest and exuberance in the performance of duty.

INITIATIVE   Taking action in the absence of orders.

INTEGRITY   Uprightness of character and soundness of moral principles.

JUDGMENT   The ability to weigh facts and possible courses of action in order to make sound decisions.

JUSTICE   Giving reward and punishment according to the merits of the case in question. The ability to administer a system of rewards and punishments impartially and consistently.

KNOWLEDGE   Understanding of a science or an art. The range of one's information, including professional knowledge and an understanding of your Marines.

LOYALTY   The quality of faithfulness to country, the Corps, and unit, and to one's seniors, subordinates, and peers.

TACT The ability to deal with others without creating hostility.

UNSELFISHNESS Avoidance of providing for one's own comfort and personal advancement at the expense of others.

....

Not all the extreme liberals are in Washington. We come across ultra-liberal characters in our daily lives in the workplace and socially. As long as they don't act out their beliefs on the social arena, we can accept each other openly. But, since character is hardwired, the extreme liberal feels impelled to change society and to push his ideas on others. (Any doubt about this aspect of the extreme liberal character will be promptly dispelled by reading Alinsky's Rules for Radicals). We have to protect ourselves from being affected by the extreme liberal's reaction when he senses that we do not share his viewpoint.

CHAPTER 11
PROTECT YOURSELF

How can we protect ourselves from the destructive person who wants to infect us with his ideas? In reality each one of us is, at one time or another, susceptible to becoming caught up in the life-negative impulses that come from another person's secondary layer. Our own secondary layer (unless we are perfect core-beings, we all have a secondary layer) can resonate with the negative impulses from another's.

Permit me to present a physician's perspective on how to protect ourselves. Consider, for a moment, the analogy that the destructive element in human character is like an infectious agent, such a virus or bacteria. Each one of us is vulnerable to being infected. We need a good immune system to protect us.

Our strongest immunity against the destructive aspect of human character comes from staying in touch with our core values.

Most things in life pull us away from our core. Daily life is a struggle as we devote most of our energy and time to making a living, supporting a family, giving to our community. We are at our most vulnerable when we are rundown and tired. We are at our most receptive to negative thoughts when we are fatigued and feel drained. At such times, we may be tempted to look to others to fix our problems. We may be tempted to accept the government's handouts, bailouts and promises of peace and prosperity. We look at the daunting issues and give into our disappointment and disillusionment as we sigh and say, "What's the use? Why fight it? Surely it's not that bad if the government decides my life for me?"

These are signs that we are vulnerable. We're more likely to catch a cold when we're rundown. At times like this, we need to take extra care by reducing our exposure to the destructive actions and agenda of others. Here are some tips to protect ourselves that I found useful personally and in my medical practice.

1. Identify and isolate the infection.

We don't expose ourselves unnecessarily to a virus. It's best to avoid the person who is sneezing and coughing hate, contempt, and nastiness. We don't try to change the mind of the extreme liberal character because we will become more frustrated and enraged. Remember, the destructive component of the extreme liberal agenda is to weaken us as an individual (by removing us from our core or making us doubt we even have a core) and to control our opinion.

2. Stay alert and be aware.

Turn off the television set. Although we are awake, too much television watching actually puts the critical reasoning part of our brain to sleep and dulls our contact with our core. The message from political talking heads on the television can seep into our brains when we are in this passive receptive state of mind.

3. Trust our feelings.

When someone pulls us away from our center, we begin to doubt ourselves. We may even begin to feel powerless and devalued. When we feel these things, it is time to return to base and connect with our strength. Ask: "Am I responding to something that comes from the core or not? Is this person's attitude life-enhancing or life-negating?" If the answer is a negative, we should see the other person's actions and ideas as an infectious agent and treat it as such by isolating it and symbolically washing our hands of the negativity to avoid being contaminated.

4. Then seek ways to get in touch with your core.

This may be a walk in the park, getting in contact with nature, working in the garden (I have a friend who finds pulling weeds very restorative), being with loved ones, attending a prayer group, or associating with like-minded core-driven individuals such as a Tea Party meeting. We find whatever works for us to reestablish core-contact.

Once we reconnect with our feelings and values that flow from the nucleus of our being, we then immerse ourselves back in the world. The next chapter gives us some ways to bolster our immunity to the destructive impulses that arise in others.

CHAPTER 12
BECOMING BATTLE-HARDY

Some people wonder all their lives if they've made a difference. The Marines don't have that problem.

~ Ronald Reagan

Like it or not, we're fighting for our survival. We are in a battle against Jihadists who kill us and try to destroy our way of life at every chance they get. We are assailed by those, who by their policies, are bankrupting and separating us from our core-values.

The threats we face are different from anything in our history because we're in as much danger from within as outside our borders.

In World War II, the British formed a "home guard" of civilian volunteers to protect home soil while their armed forces fought overseas. In the same way, we have a National Guard to safeguard us on American soil, and our Constitution empowers the people to form a militia, with the right to bear arms. We have a strong, courageous military to protect us and engage the enemy but, more than ever, we need a home guard armed with core values.

**The brave men and women of our Armed Forces
need us to watch their backs at home.**

The first step in becoming a warrior is to go through boot camp where we're given a crash course in core values and strength. Boot camp transforms us from one life into another and instills values that will stand the test of hardship and battle.

In a similar way, we citizens have to be tough enough to protect our nation and core values. This means being core-hardy and self-reliant. Here are some of the boot camp principles, which I refer to as the 6 C's, that will keep us strong. These ideas are based on the work of psychologist Susan Kobasa who identified the concept of stress hardiness.

The 6 C's to becoming core-hardy:

1. Comparison
2. Challenge
3. Control
4. Commitment
5. Closeness
6. Character

1. Core-value comparison

We compare everything to our core values. Our core values are the yardstick by which we compare all other values. By determining the degree to which they are life-enhancing or life-weakening we can measure how far they are from our core values. In this way we can readily see if anyone is asking us to move away from our center.

We don't compare or judge by outward appearances but by the fruits, the results of the actions. If we do this, we won't be blinded by empty promises and clever words.

Our feelings alert us when we are being tugged from our core-center. Moving away from our core feels like swimming upstream against the direction of life. It's an effort that makes us feel weaker, less resilient and less creative. We don't like it when we are asked to go in the opposite direction of greater freedom and responsibility, work and fulfillment. To relinquish our core is to devalue our individuality and become weak and vulnerable.

We can ask the following questions in any situation, political or otherwise. Our feeling in response to the questions gives us our answer:

- Is this life positive?

- Will it strengthen me?

- Does it promote and respect the individual or would it make me subservient to the government?

- Does it protect my freedom?

- Will it make our enemies fear us?

2. Challenge

Adversity is a challenge. Whenever we encounter an obstacle in the path, we have a choice whether to give up or see it as a challenge to be overcome. The extreme liberal wants us to give up, to become helpless and depend on the state. It's easier to drift with the current and to be pulled along by the tsunami of rules and regulations than it is to assert our individuality against the government. It's an almost overwhelming task to change the scope and focus of big government. It is like encountering a huge boulder on our path of individual freedom. We can shrug our shoulders and say, "What can I do, as an individual?" Or we can take up the challenge to consolidate and preserve our freedom.

Once we accept a challenge, we engage our core which gives us the tools we need. Our core generates the energy, drive and our sense of purpose and recruits others to join forces with us to meet the challenge.

An interesting study published in a medical journal in 1968 described how a sense of challenge determines the way we react to extreme stress. A small group of special force Green Berets was stationed in an isolated camp near the Cambodian border in South Vietnam. They were outnumbered, outgunned and anticipated an overwhelming hostile attack. A scientist among them collected blood and urine samples from the soldiers to measure chemicals that indicate the body's response to stress. He expected to find high levels of adrenaline and cortisol, the chemical markers of stress. Instead he found the opposite. The curve was flat because these hardened soldiers regarded the imminent attack as a challenge to be met with courage and resolve, and doing so engaged their core strength.

We can take a lesson from these Green Berets not only in accepting the challenge to reverse the bankrupting of our society but in every aspect of our daily lives.

3. Control

We cannot change the big picture overnight but we can start at the individual and local level for the right to control our own personal lives. Feeling that we have little or no control over our lives creates an enormous amount of stress and leads to a negative defeatist attitude. Why do we think big government wants to assume control of our health care decision-making, what we should eat and so on? The present political battle is largely a fight for us to submit control of our life, piece by piece, to the government.

At every level we encounter those who want to make our decisions for us, be it at on the school board, work, city council and all way up to the federal government. Relinquishing control of our own personal choice is the first step towards dependency and helplessness. We have to choose our fights and decide what we can control and what we cannot. Our core tells us this difference and is the basis of the serenity prayer:

"God grant me the serenity
to accept the things I cannot change;
courage to change the things I can;
and wisdom to know the difference."

4. Commitment

Once we embark on a task, we have to see it through for it to be successful.

One of the biggest lessons from the War of Independence was the demonstration of the power of commitment and perseverance. Although General Washington's army was in tatters, weak, hungry and frostbitten, they endured and persisted to eventual victory. Their prospects looked hopeless and bleak, but they never gave up.

Likewise, we cannot give up fighting to preserve our liberty. Our need to persevere applies equally to domestic, social and political issues as it does to the protracted war against the Islamic fascists. In this way we don't look for quick fixes – we've been promised too many of these before.

5. Closeness/colleagues/coworkers/co-patriots

No man is an island. We are much stronger when we can lean on others in adversity, and our joy is much greater when shared. The army squad commander knows that his men support one another and that morale depends on this cohesiveness. The public speaker is less nervous if he has a friend or family member in the audience.

On the same principle as enunciated in the Bible "when two or more are gathered in my name", we know that when two or more people join in the service of life and truth, an invisible, powerful and uplifting factor kicks in. The whole becomes much greater than the sum of its parts. In this light, we can see why the extreme liberal tries to divide us and split us apart. The deliberate polarization and fragmentation of our society is to weaken us, to make us vulnerable and dependent.

We look around for people who feel like we do, who share similar core values. If the mainstream political parties disappoint us, if we don't belong to a temple or church, we can join a Tea Party or a citizen group. In this way, by being with others who have similar life-positive goals, we add to the power of the whole.

Let's not sit alone in front of the television or computer screen shaking our heads and feeling helpless. There's too much at stake.

6. Character

While the importance of understanding political character cannot be stressed enough, the word character also describes an inner strength. A strong character is stable under stress and is undeterred by adversity or disappointment. He holds on to his values and does not change with the prevailing wind. He can defer gratification until he gets the job done. A strong character is self confident and does not depend on the approval of others. He is dependable under fire. You want this person in your foxhole.

Chapter 13
Pitfalls and Strengths as we Move Forward

Be always sure you're right, then go ahead.

~ Davy Crockett

Although the 2010 midterm election shows that the leftward drift is beginning to reverse itself, more than ever before, we need to avoid sliding back into the same old "business as usual" that got us into the present mess. This chapter includes some of the mistakes we don't want to repeat as we move our country back to center. It also highlights the traits that will keep us strong. Here are the things we have to be aware of in the road ahead:

1. Ignoring character
2. Complacency
3. Accountability
4. Responsibility
5. Unity
6. Strength
7. Fear of speaking out
8. KISS
9. Management by crisis
10. The cult of personality
11. Entitlement
12. The danger of extremism

1. Ignoring character

Arguably, the most important lesson of the 2008 elections is that we were taken in by Barack Obama's gloss, smile and intellectual brilliance, and we ignored his character.

I recall attending a seminar on character analysis. Among the attendees who were physicians, mostly psychiatrists, there was one person who was not a medic. By using his understanding of character, this attorney was more able to know his clients, read his adversaries and, ultimately, win big cases. In the same way, being willing to see a person's political character is extremely valuable for those of us who are trying to decide who we should trust with our money, security and future. In 2008, as a nation, we were bamboozled by the glare of charisma and empty promises while we ignored the red flags of the extreme liberal character. The importance of evaluating a person's political character applies to members of all political parties because character is more important than political affiliation.

From now on, we should judge every political candidate against our core values and hold each elected official to his sworn duty to protect and preserve our core document, the Constitution.

2. Complacency

To be complacent is to be satisfied with an existing situation while being unaware of a potential danger. We are at risk for becoming complacent if we are satisfied with the conservative gains in the recent mid-term elections because it's only the beginning of a long slow struggle to regain our core values as a nation. We would have learned nothing if we believe that either political party will adhere to core values unless we hold them to it. Power corrupts, and what begins as a politician's good intentions often ends up not being in the people's best interest. Our complacency leads to loss of accountability when we don't hold our elected officials to their promises.

3. Accountability

The people we elected to power on a conservative or back-to-center platform need our help and support to retain their core base because the influences in Washington will pull them away from their core. The compromising of values and the self-interest that pervades Washington are forces from the secondary layer that will tug a person, no matter how strong he is, away from his core. This time around, we will remind our representatives of their platforms and promises and support them in their battle to adhere to their core values. We erred in not holding our elected officials accountable for their actions and inactions and by waiting only until Election Day to act.

4. Responsibility

The elected official, be he a school board member, a state representative or even the president bears the responsibility to use his power in the interest of the people. It is not the politician's money to spread around, to buy favors. We allowed irresponsible core-less politicians to squander our wealth. Power corrupts at all levels. The citizens of Bell, California were jolted awake from their stupor to find that their city officials had stolen them blind. The townspeople reacted too late to prevent loss of local services, but their outrage led to the ousting and arrest of these self-serving officials who they had once trusted. As a nation, some of us are now waking up to the same things at the federal level, and we are beginning to identify and replace those politicians who show no evidence of being able to function from their core.

5. Unity

The ploy of "divide and rule" is used to weaken our will in opposing the progressive agenda. As a nation we all have a shared interest in moving back to center and reclaiming our strength and solvency based on core values. Liberals and conservatives can agree to differ as long as the differences center on core values. In this way we avoid polarization and extremism, which weakens us further. Our mistake was allowing ourselves to be divided from each other and alienated from our individual and collective core. Much of the talk of bipartisanship was a setup because the extreme liberal character has no intention of compromising his agenda. The political polarization and rage infects the whole country as toxic ideas and ideology go viral.

6. Strength

We permitted weakness to replace strength. We made the mistake of being fooled by appeasement disguised by good intentions and humanitarian gestures. By holding true to core values, we are less likely to make the same mistake again. To evaluate our leaders' strength we can look at which of the 14 leadership traits (summarized in the appendix) they show.

7. Fear of speaking out

Speaking the truth will help reverse the paralyzing effect of political correctness that stifles expression of our opinions and the right to disagree. If we don't express what we know in an open and honest way, our own truth will eventually become alien to us. Our mistake was to allow a culture of political correctness to prevent us from expressing our core values.

8. KISS (keep it simple stupid).

We believed we could not understand the major issues because we were told they were too complicated for us.

When things become overly complex for us to understand, we feel vulnerable and have to rely on experts who can twist the facts to suit their beliefs and agenda. The complexity of issues obscured the truth of the hyped up global warming "crisis" as well as the financial "crisis."

Forgive me for repeating this, but it is so important:

The closer the truth something is, the more simple it becomes.

Even if we don't understand the ins and outs of science or economics, we can look at how the issue relates to core values. Do they make sense? Does the proposed response strengthen or weaken us? We test everything against our core values and follow those feelings that will tell us whether it is life-positive or life-negative. For expert opinions, we can turn to trusted resources such as the Cato Institute or the Heritage Society for a balanced and core-based analysis.

9. Management by crisis

Our mistaken belief in a healthcare "crisis" allowed the extreme liberals to avoid transparency and circumvent public debate. Remember how a sense of urgency and crisis confused us and how we suspended judgment and looked to our leaders to direct us. We need to ask, "How bad is this crisis? Is the proposed response to this crisis one that furthers a particular agenda or does it restore balance, strength and wealth?" A true crisis, an emergency or threat engages our core (as did those Green Berets and as we did as a nation following the September 11 attacks) whereas a false manipulated crisis displaces us from our core. Now that we know the difference, we won't be as easily blinded again by a fabricated sense of crisis.

10. The cult of personality

Since we live in a media-driven culture of personality, screen idols and celebrities, we become so accustomed to the superficial layer that we easily confuse the façade with the real character. President Obama's personality, heavily promoted by the media, obscured his character. Even now, at the time of writing this book, opinion polls show that while the majority of Americans don't like President Obama's policies, they still like him "as a person." A soulful, honest and direct person is seldom interesting to the media. The media feasts on the secondary layer, not the core.

Will we make the same mistake again with the next crop of political candidates?

11. Entitlement

We made the mistake of encouraging a sense of entitlement. Entitlement is a trap because once we receive something in return for nothing, we expect the benefits to continue. The demonstrations that erupted in Greece, in Spain, and France when the government tried to take back some of the entitlements show how hard it is to take a freebie back once it is given. Almost half of all US citizens pay no federal income tax, yet many receive benefits from the state. Many of those who do so feel that it is their right to receive something for nothing. The official government term for these programs is "entitlement programs," which were designed to help those in true need and to provide a safety net.

We won't make the same mistake if we refer to our core values and differentiate between assisting those in need from the expectation of getting something for nothing.

12. The danger of extremism

The danger of extremism always lurks in the background on the left and on the right. Extremism feeds on crisis, fear and uncertainty. Let us be suspicious of extreme views and quick fix solutions offered by people who have absolutely no contact with their core.

Conclusion

We're beginning to realize how dangerously far we have drifted from our core values. The spontaneous banding together of concerned citizens outside of the two major political parties is unique in modern times. These movements are a response to the betrayal by politicians, in both political parties, of our core values. This groundswell from the people is not really a political movement because our focus is on defining and reclaiming core values as enunciated in our Constitution. We must remain aware that such movements can become politicized and institutionalized.

We can reclaim center by carefully selecting candidates for office based on their character and how they relate to core values no matter what their political party.

Reversing the harmful shift away from core is the beginning of a long protracted task, but, if we persevere, we will succeed beyond our wildest dreams. America is fertile soil for the entrepreneur, for those with imagination and drive, and for the expression of all core values. No other country in the world has a Constitution so centered on such clearly stated core values. If we core-reclaimers persevere through multiple election cycles to come, we can restore the true character of our country. To do so, those of us who cherish and value our core, need to:

- Identify those who seek political power who function close to their core

- Support them in our joint struggle to regain our center

- Hold elected officials to their promises and pledges

- Rally around the only core document this country has, the Constitution

- Speak the truth and make it acceptable to do so

- Withstand the hate-filled attacks of those who are threatened by truth and by core values.

A Final Perspective: *The "Truth-Teller"*

Throughout history the person who reveals himself and openly expresses his core truth has been vilified and crucified by those around him who are threatened by truth. This unfortunate fact is as true today as it was in the biblical times.

Why then would any core-character choose to enter the realm of politics and expose himself to those who will attack him and put his values and reputation at risk?

We can change the toxic atmosphere if we support the political candidate who openly shares our values and if we support him in his battle to express his values on the political scene. He is no longer alone as we draw on our core values to change the political arena from a lonely life-negating environment into a life-positive scene.

The appendices list the core values, traits of the core character and the 14 leadership traits as quick reminders. These are our rules of engagement for asserting our core values.

God Bless America

APPENDICES

Additional reading

17-0HCS Levels in Combat. Special Forces "A" Team Under Threat of Attack. Peter G. Bourne, Robert M. Rose, John W. Mason) Archives General Psychiatry 19:135-140, 1968 (the study that shows what core strength really is in combat)

Personality and Constitution as Mediators in the Stress-Illness Relationship. Suzanne C. Kobasa, Salvatore R. Maddi and Sheila Courington. Journal of Health and Social Behavior Vol. 22, No. 4 (Dec., 1981), pp. 368-378 (the psychological basis for stress hardiness)

Saul D. Alinsky. Rules for Radicals. A Practical Primer for Realistic Radicals. Vintage, 1989 (this book, first published in 1971, set the rules for community organizing)

E. F. Baker. Man in the Trap. New York: Macmillan, 1967 (a psychiatry textbook that includes the first known description of the political character types)

James Burnham. Suicide of the West: An Essay on the Meaning and Destiny of Liberalism. Regnery Publishing, 1985 (this collection of essays, first publishes in 1964, is a chilling predictor of what happens with unchecked liberal power)

Jonah Goldberg. Liberal Fascism: The Secret History of the American Left, From Mussolini to the Politics of Meaning. New York: Doubleday, 2008 (this book includes the remarkable observation of how extreme liberals and extreme conservatives begin to resemble each other)

Charles Konia. The Emotional Plague. The Root of Human Evil. Princeton: ACO press, 2008 (a psychiatry textbook that examines the origin of human destructive behavior)

Mark R. Levin. Liberty and Tyranny: A Conservative Manifesto. New York: Threshold Editions, 2009 (a timely book on the battle between conservative and liberal forces in our society)

Wilhelm Reich. The Mass Psychology of Fascism. New York: Farrar, Straus and Giroux, 1970 (first published in 1933, this is a classic evaluation of the origin of Fascism from a psychiatric point of view)

Thomas Sowell. Dismantling America: and other controversial essays. Basic Books, 2010 (a well-respected economist's view of the gradual destruction of our society)

Quick reminders

Feelings from our core

- Feeling of belonging, being part of life and nature
- Religious feeling, acknowledging an inner wisdom, a power higher than our own
- Love of life and respect for life
- Respect for the individual
- Love of freedom and liberty but not without the responsibility that it entails
- Simplicity rather than complexity
- Love of work
- Custody and a sense of responsibility for the environment
- Belief in the intrinsic goodness of man but still able to recognize and respond to the destructive impulse in others

Core Values

- Value of freedom and liberty but not without the responsibility that it entails
- Strength and resolve to protect life
- Placing value on the core of others (loving your neighbor as your self)
- Value of work
- Respect for the individual
- Attitude of live and let live

- No desire to impose our will or opinions on others
- Independence
- Feeling of custodianship and responsibility for the environment
- Ability to recognize and respond to the destructive actions of others
- Respect for the life-positive beliefs of others, including their religious beliefs
- Love and respect for life in all its manifestations

Leadership Qualities

Bearing

Courage

Decisiveness

Dependability

Endurance

Enthusiasm

Initiative

Integrity

Judgment

Justice

Knowledge

Loyalty

Tact

Unselfishness

Summary of the Differences between the Conservative and Liberal Character

Priorities

- Conservative: prioritizes freedom and liberty (Freedom > liberty > justice > peace)

- Liberal: values peace and justice first, even at the expense of freedom (peace > justice > liberty > freedom)

Head vs. heart

- Conservative: retains feeling from the core, tends to be less intellectual. Is more open, direct and forthright.

- Liberal: lives more in the world of ideas and words. Has less contact with his core feelings. Tends to use the intellect as a weapon.

Importance of the individual

- Conservative: places high value on the individual

- Liberal: places less value on the individual, and greater emphasis on society as a whole

Responsibility

- Conservative: has a strong sense of responsibility, being responsible for one's own actions.

- Liberal: has less sense of personal responsibility and tends to displace responsibility onto the state

Aggression

- Conservative: is more capable of natural aggression in defense of values and vulnerable life. He is able to distinguish between healthy aggression (from the core) and destructive aggression that comes from the secondary layer.

- Liberal: essentially, he is not able to tolerate aggression and will go to great lengths to avoid it. The liberal finds it difficult to distinguish between healthy and destructive aggression.

Privilege

- Conservative: sees privilege as earned and deserved

- Liberal: regards privilege as a right

Religious feeling

- Conservative: retains feeling for life and a power greater than himself.

- Liberal: downplays or even ignores religious feelings in favor of ideas

Patriotism

- Conservative: is strongly patriotic and believes in American exceptionalism

- Liberal: disdains patriotism and he sees all people as the same

The Constitution

- Conservative: believes strongly in the Constitution as a template for core values

- Liberal: sees the Constitution as open to change and to be reinterpreted according to modern times

Government

- Conservative: believes in limited central government and strong local government closer to the individual
- Liberal: believes in the power and wisdom of central government for the greater good of society

Education

- Conservative: sees that education is for learning and acquiring life skills. Grades are to be earned and deserved.
- Liberal: stresses the importance of group thinking, social studies. He places less emphasis on individual responsibility and encourages promotion regardless of grades.

Reaction when challenged

- Conservative: tends to be more naïve, open, direct and confrontational
- Liberal: tends to use his intellect and becomes sarcastic, derisive, contemptuous with personal attacks

Peace at any price

- Conservative: pacifism is anathema to the conservative.
- Liberal: appeasement and yielding in the face of aggression are common liberal responses to an enemy. The liberal believes that because people are inherently good, they can be persuaded by reason and arguments

Capitalism

- Conservative: is attracted to free enterprise and reward for hard work

- Liberal: sees the capitalist system as unfair to the lesser man. He seeks a leveling to reduce competition and believes that wealth should be shared, regardless of worth or work.

Charity

- Conservative: has genuine concern for the disadvantaged but wants to select his charity of choice

- Liberal: thinks that the state should decide who to support, not the individual

Perception - how we see the world

- Conservative: tends to see things more realistically

- Liberal: tends to see things as he thinks they should be

Remember a conservative character may have liberal views but, under stress, will respond according to his character. In contrast, it is less common for a liberal character to hold conservative views.

Guideposts

- Look at the motive behind the action and words

- Look at the fruit of the actions, the results

- Never take anything at face value

- If you have any doubt, return to your core and core values and test what you see against these values and your feelings.

- Remember, truth and guidance is found in your inner self, your core.

- Associate with others who share similar core values.

Self-test Questions

Let's see if our understanding of political character types helps us to answer these questions.

Regarding the McCain - Palin campaign of 2008:

> Why was Sarah Palin attacked in such a personal and hateful manner?
> Who do you think is the conservative of the two?
> Is John McCain really a conservative character?

Why have conservatives from Ronald Reagan through Bush been cast as stupid?

Why do political contenders such as Mitt Romney have to downplay their religious identity?

Has the Republican Party strayed to the left?

Can you identify any liberal characters in the Republican Party?

Can you identify any conservative characters in the Democratic Party?

Why did we tolerate the appointment of a treasury secretary who cheated on his taxes?

Why do so few Muslims speak out against the extreme Islamo-fascisits?

What are the real motives for wanting to build a mosque at ground zero?

What power do we the people really have?

Which character, liberal or conservative, in politics is most likely to have had a real job or run a business?

This one is for you history buffs. Were there liberal characters among the framers of our Constitution?

Can you explain why the polls show that while the majority of Americans dislike president Obama's policies they admire him as a person?

Why did the majority of legislators vote on the health-care bill without reading it?

How many crises have we had since President Obama took office?

Are we Americans, as a people, basically liberal or conservative characters?

Why do think there is a geographical difference in the distribution of conservative and liberal characters in this country?

What indicators were there of Barack Obama's character before the election?

How do you view his character now compared to during his election campaign?

Why do some accuse the Tea Party movement of being racist?

Do some in the Republican Party feel threatened by the tea party movement? If so, why?

Why was Scott Brown's election in Massachusetts such a surprise?

Do you feel that president Obama can change his attitude to the capitalist free enterprise system?

How do you feel about being punished if you don't have health-insurance?

Why do only 11% of the American people have any confidence in their representatives in Washington?

Why do the majority of Americans now want Obamacare repealed?

www.ingramcontent.com/pod-product-compliance
Lightning Source LLC
Chambersburg PA
CBHW072201280526
45788CB00002B/827